I'VE USED ALL MY SICK DAYS . . .

now I'll have to call in dead!

Cindi Wood

I'VE USED ALL MY SICK DAYS
Now I'll Have To Call In Dead

Copyright 1998
Cindi Wood

Third Printing
February 1999

ISBN: 1-890736-05-8

Drawbridge Publishing
PO Box 1010
Kings Mountain, NC 28086

Printed in the USA by

MORRIS PUBLISHING

3212 East Highway 30 • Kearney, NE 68847 • 1-800-650-7888

Larry -- Brandon -- Lane

This book is lovingly dedicated to my husband and sons who have made me everything I am today ~ FRAZZLED!

Because of them I almost didn't finish writing this book. But without them, there would not have been a reason to write!

Oh! How I love you guys!!

In Appreciation

If all the events which have caused me to be sick (and on some occasions almost dead), had proper names, I'd thank each and every one of them right now.

Instead I give thanks to my Heavenly Father ~ who in His permissive will, has allowed turbulence in my life so that I might grow in the desire to help others, as I grow in intimacy with Him.

To God be the glory!

Cindi Wood
March 1998

A Special Thank You ~

Goes to my older son Brandon, who knows how to put his mom's words into pictures.

Thanks Honey, for spreading your wit and humor throughout the pages of this book. You are truly the sharpest pencil in the pack!

Thanks ~

For the insights provided by those faithful employees in Kings Mountain, Shelby, and Cleveland County Schools. I also thank you ladies who work in the world outside of the school system.

A galaxy of thanks to the "Princesses of the King" Sunday School Class. Your love, support, and encouragement have been an icon of strength for me during these past months.

Another thank-you to my long-time buddy and colleague Pat Jobe, who is a mericless (I mean merciless) editor. Pat, your gifts of wit, wisdom, and time, are truly appreciated by this gal.

Contents:

INTRODUCTION

What happens **to** us doesn't matter as much as what happens **in** us!

The scores of women I have encountered throughout my years of workshop training, keynote speaking, and seminar presentations ~ have taught me this truth.

Life happens. It just happens. We don't have control over many of the circumstances that come our way. We certainly don't have control over other people. But we DO have control of ourselves.

Your life is an extension of your thoughts. Thoughts are powerful. They can lead you to crumble under guilt, worry, confusion, and erosion of mind and body. They can also energize you and help you learn to creatively manage the stresses of life. The choice is yours!

Sick and tired of being sick and tired?!?

Well, cruise on through the following pages. You are not alone. Seems that women everywhere who are living on the twentieth century fast-track are looking for ways to get off the ever-speeding treadmill for a rest.

It isn't that we want to give up many of the things we are involved in. We just want to keep our sanity in the middle of all the chaos!

I'm reminded of a time before our boys were born. It was a carefree day at the mall, enjoying shopping and people watching.

Then SHE appeared . . . Wonder Woman, Super Mom, and the Bionic Woman, three in one ~ bouncing out of the elevator on the second floor with two charming children, one on each hand. Oh, they certainly were the picture of happiness. My heart yearned for motherhood and shopping with my children.

Five years later, I had to solder the leash off my first son's arm, and nine years after that, repeated the same procedure with his little brother. I didn't take them anywhere without that elastic band snuggly fastened around their little wrists, and I'm still looking for that woman to find out where she got those kids!

There's a point or two here. First, we don't always know, nor can we predict, what's going to come our way. Secondly, when the "unexpected" arrives, strap on the leash and move with the flow.

Those years, although not exactly how I had pictured them before having children, are some of the most delightful memories I have of being a "mommy". Skipping, singing, and dancing throughout the mall made some happy memories for all of us.

(An interesting side-note here is the realization of how one's perspective can change. Being an educator and knowing ALL about children and their behaviors ~ and besides that, being a very self-respecting and dignified woman, I would NEVER had entertained the notion of putting MY children on a leash. Those were used by other women who did not know how to control children . . .)

Alas . . . my plans changed. I learned early in my mothering years to adapt to the ever-changing (usually quite unexpected) circumstances, make the best of the situation and move with the flow.

It's a process. It's a challenge. It's a choice!

My desire is that you will find some tools in this book to help you adapt to what comes your way, make the best of your circumstances, and build memories - mostly happy ones!

ATTENTION: ALL PERSONNEL
SUBJECT: EXCESSIVE ABSENCES

THE FOLLOWING RULES ARE IN EFFECT:

SICKNESS
Absolutely no excuses. We will no longer accept your doctor's statement as proof, as we believe that if you are able to go to the doctor, you are able to come to work.

LEAVE OF ABSENCE FOR AN OPERATION
We are no longer allowing this practice. We wish to discourage any thoughts that you may need an operation, as we believe that as long as you are an employee here you will need all of whatever you have, and you should not consider having anything removed. We hired you as you are and to have anything removed would certainly make you less than we bargained for.

ACCIDENTS
Our safety programs and company policy preclude any lost time for accidents. First aid in most instances will be treated during normal breaks. Application of splints, hemorrhage and artificial respiration may be done at other times, work load permitting.

DEATH (YOUR OWN)
This will be accepted as an excuse, but a two week notice is required as we feel it is your duty to teach someone else your job.

THE OFFICE HUMOR BOOK

Improving Your Attitude

1

I once read that we individuals are functioning at only a fraction of our potentials, not because of lack of skills or knowledge, but because of our attitudes.

That must be true of our lives in general. Relationships among family and friends, personal pursuits of success, physical health, and time spent with one's self, hold infinitely greater possibilities for most people if they will only make some adjustments in their attitudes.

If we change our inner attitudes, we can change many of the outer aspects of our lives!

So ~ how's YOUR attitude today?

It depends on **what day it is,** most women respond. A positive attitude can have a remarkably short half-life, many of us have noticed.

 Women are usually pretty vulnerable to mood swings. Blame it on emotions, hormones, or just BEING WOMAN!

Research has shown that we are much more emotional than our male counterparts, as well as tending to focus more on negative moods and to worry about them. That even makes the moods worse.

Take a few minutes to test your positive thinking quotient. This quiz taken from The <u>Complete Guide To Your Emotions and Your Health</u>, will give you an idea of where you rank on the winner's attitude scale.

Answer the 15 questions as honestly as possible, using this scoring system: In the margin, put a 5 if your answer is Always or Almost Always; 4 if it's Usually; 3 for Sometimes; 2 for Rarely; 1 for Never.

When the unexpected forces you to change your plans, are you quick to spot a hidden advantage in this new situation?

When you catch a stranger staring at you, do you conclude it's because he or she finds you attractive?

Do you like most of the people you meet?

When you think about next year, do you tend to think you'll be better off then than you are now?

Do you often stop to admire things of beauty?

When someone finds fault with you or something you've done, can you tell the difference between useful criticism and "sour grapes," which is better off ignored?

Do you praise your spouse/best friend more often than you criticize him or her?

Do you believe the human race will survive well into the twenty-first century?

Are you surprised when a friend lets you down?

Do you think you are happy?

If a policeman stopped you for speeding when you were quite certain you weren't, would you firmly argue your case and even take it to court to prove you were right?

Do you feel comfortable making yourself the butt of your own jokes?

Do you believe that, overall, your state of mind has had a positive effect on your physical health?

If you made a list of your ten favorite people, would you be on it?

When you think back over the past few months, do you tend to remember your little successes before your setbacks and failures?

Now score.

If you scored 65 or over, consider yourself a "superstar" -- someone whose optimism is a powerful, healing force.

60-65: Excellent -- you're a genuine positive thinker.

55-60: Good -- you're a positive thinker, sometimes.

50-55: Fair -- your positive side and your negative side are about evenly matched.

50 and below: Do you see any consistent negative patterns? Where could you improve?

So how did you do?

We all have our tendencies towards a certain temperament and attitude. Depending upon experiential and environmental factors, we tend to look at situations either positively or negatively.

We also evolve into a behavioral style that causes us to be cautious, skeptical, and looking on the "negative possibility" side, **or** generally risk-taking, high energy, and hoping for the best in whatever the situation.

Regardless of our environment and style of behavior, positive and negative thinkers aren't born that way. We develop habits over years of absorbing the attitudes of those around us ~ parents, teachers, peers, even TV figures.

Day after day, week after week, messages are being encoded in our minds. Over the course of a day, we carry on conversations with ourselves, interpret situations, and cast judgements.

Now, this self-talk can be explosions of doubt and criticism like, "I know I'll never be able to complete this project"; "I know I'm not good enough to . . . ."; "No one can be trusted."

Or we can feed ourselves positive messages.
"Things will work out"; "I know I can handle this situation"; "I'm good at what I do", are positive reinforcements to our self esteem.

You feel the way you think.

Explore the scenarios on the following pages:

After coming up with a brilliant idea at work which will help all involved manage their time more effectively, you are highly commended and praised. Do you feel A) proud and deserving of the praise, knowing that continued effort could lead to a promotion or B) awkward and apologetic, explaining that the idea was by chance and will probably be the only one you'll ever have.

When a car pulls out several feet in front of you, there is a near collision. Do you feel A) relieved and grateful that it missed you or B) upset and distraught by your near catastrophe?

A family member is undergoing chemotherapy for cancer. Do you feel A) reassured, an indication that your loved one is getting state-of the-art medical care or B) disturbed by the treatment because it is a reminder of your loved one's fragile state of health?

Whether you chose the positive A answers or the more negative B ones, these illustrations lead us to a realization: Situations don't change your attitudes. Your perception of them does.

Your attitudes have a profound effect on your physical, mental, and emotional health. People who are constantly worrying and viewing their lives in negative terms, work themselves into a state of low self-esteem and depression.

Every time you think the worst, your body and mind react with tension and stress. Your pulse rate quickens and the adrenaline flows. If you continue to dwell on these negative thoughts, you'll become exhausted and depleted. Add to that headaches, stomach problems, and other stress-related physical ailments.

On the other hand, a positive attitude produces positive results. Positive thinking builds up your self-confidence, your day-to-day living, your success, and even your health.

Women with winning attitudes generally build on their strengths, work on their weaknesses, and develop a mindset to put up with the rain until the rainbow appears.

Steps to viewing the rainbow:

1) **Act. Don't brood.** If you feel an "attitude coming on", do something. Take a walk, clear the clutter off your desk. Do something that puts YOU in control and gives you a sense of accomplishment.

2) **Think rationally.** A negative attitude can siphon your energy and cause your thinking to be distorted. Are there alternative ways of thinking about this situation? What's the worse that could happen, and how would you deal, if it did?

3) **Grab some mood food.** An all-carbohydrate snack like a cinnamon-raisin bagel can turn on those calming neurotransmitters in your brain.

4) **Start exercising.** It has so many physiological and psychological benefits. Exercise prompts your brain to release a natural feel-good substance called serotonin. Research shows that women who exercise regularly feel more enthusiastic, energetic, and upbeat.

5) **Do something for You.** Don't feel selfish about it. Doing something for yourself reinforces the idea that you are worthwhile. Doing something that makes you feel good will help your attitude improve and give you a better outlook on life. Begin by doing something this very day. Make an appointment to get your nails done, for example. Get a tension relieving neck massage, or go out to dinner with a special friend (and while you're giggling and telling stories, try to eat at least a little.)

6) **Talk nicely to yourself.** Taking note of your good qualities and giving yourself positive affirmations will help you appreciate the good qualities in others.

7) **Smile.** It sets the tempo for the day. It's a way of splashing your thoughts on your face. Smile for your family. Smile for those at work. Make it a happy day for you and those around you.

Attitude Warranty

Guarantee:
Be in control of the way you get up and get started in the morning ~ and you will change your life for the better!

Guarantee:
If you look for the good in other people and situations ~ you will discover the gold and not the dirt!

Guarantee:
Learn how to greet and respond to people cheerfully ~ and you will become more cheerful!

Guarantee:
Take care of yourself physically ~ and you will enjoy the benefits of good health!

Guarantee:
If you make plenty of positive deposits into your mind ~ you will be able to make more positive withdrawals!

Managing Your Time

Have you ever

considered the fact~

that one seventh of your

lifetime is spent on

Mondays ~ ugh!!!

2

I recently read about several studies dealing with time management. According to these reports, the average worker in America is productive about 54 percent of the time. If that's true, then most of us are certainly working at less than our full potential.

We're not only failing to accomplish what we could, we are creating problems for ourselves, our families and the people we work with.

To be productive, efficient, not to speak of being fulfilled; today's woman must be a master
(or mistress) of time management!

When I ask the question in my seminars, "What frazzles you in your life?", in the top three consistently is the response, "Not enough time."

Women everywhere are juggling many roles and finding that there seems to be insufficient time to be really good at any of them. We are homemakers, wives, mothers, business women, and the list goes on and on. The amount of tasks within a given day is increasing while the number of hours in one day stays the same.

It's my belief that before you can tackle a problem effectively, you must clearly define the problem. Is the problem, "I don't have enough time," or "I have too much to do."?

We keep adding things to our already frenzied life-style, forgetting that More is not always Better. When there's more and more to do, something has to give.

As a result, many women fall into the lopsided wheel trap. They get all wrapped up in one aspect of their lives (career, civic involvement, church, etc.) so deeply that nothing else is significant.

They become compulsive in that particular area while losing the balance in the other areas of life. It's very easy to do.

Picture a bicycle wheel with spokes. If the spokes are equally matched, the wheel is balanced. If not, one can expect a wreck (or at least a very bumpy ride.)

Use your visualization skills now. Let's say that these spokes are labeled FAMILY, WORK, SELF-TIME, HOUSEWORK, CHURCH, etc. Label them according to your lifestyle at this particular time of life.

Is your wheel rounded, lopsided, maybe square?!? Are there one or two areas getting most of your attention while other areas suffer?

I find that many women, because of extremely hectic schedules, neglect time for self. When this important area is overlooked, we become bitter, resentful, and often turn into martyrs.

By taking time for self we gain a sense of control, as well as reap the rewards of exercise, building relationships, improving skills, etc.

So how do we go about rounding-out this wheel and getting (and keeping) our life in balance?

We manage. Managing time means accepting its passage and re-ordering our worlds in some satisfying manner. It means managing ourselves. Time management is really self management.

Since most of us would agree that we have ***too much to do and not enough time to do it,*** we must make tough choices about what to do and what not to do.

If time seems to be out of control, it really means WE are out of control. To bring balance back, we must develop some new and appropriate habits.

You see time is not adaptable, but people are. So if we develop good habits to help us with this time dilemma, we'll see some good results.

We must keep in mind, also, that habits are learned behavior. We must practice them and remember that we are definitely in control of them. Our success in developing these positive habits depends on us.

As we begin exploring "time saving" strategies, keep in mind that a positive attitude about getting better at managing your time is vitally important. Henry Ford put it this way: "Whether you think you can or you can't, you're right."

In order to more effectively manage your time, you must want to change some things. Desire is where it all begins.

You will find also, that when you begin to manage time in one area of your life, a positive impact is made in other areas. They are all related. (For example, learning to manage clutter and paperwork at the office will help you to manage clutter and paperwork at home.)

How long does it take? Research has shown that it takes about three weeks to "cement" a new habit. You will find that consistency in this new venture really pays off.

Get Ready! Get Set! Go!

Stop talking about doing it later; do it now. Better time management is just a habit away!

As you begin thinking about changes you would like to make in your daily routine, you will want to follow this approach:

Identify the habit you want to change.

Define the new habit to go in its place.

Begin the new behavior strong and soon.

Be consistent until the habit is established.

Celebrate your successes.

TIME FLIES

In a lifetime we spend:

7 years in the bathroom
5 years in line (most of them in the
  grocery store)
3 years messing with our hair
2 years searching for "stuff"
1 year sorting through clutter

In a month we use up:

10 hours cleaning up somebody's mess
5 hours explaining things
3 hours saying "no" to sales calls

In a week we spend:

Too many hours with chores
Not enough hours on ourselves
And are interrupted 576 different times

Let's take a look at some time management habits that you may like to implement at work (and on the homefront).

1) **Handle each piece of mail once.** Take it, read it, decide whether to take further action, or trash it. It works! You'd be surprised how much time you'd save by not piling up a stack to go through later.

2) **If you receive a memo that demands a reply from you; whether it's a paragraph written or a question answered, do it right then.** First of all, you probably won't lose it, and secondly, you won't add to your stress a pack of little things to be taken care of whenever you get around to doing so. An added bonus to this system is that you appear to be so TOGETHER and organized to the people around you! Such a simple skill to live by ~ once you've mastered it.

3) **When you receive a note that needs a response, decide which is more expedient; a phone call, e-mail, fax, or a note.** Then do it. Often, the load is lessened by just picking up the phone and answering a question ~ or giving a response.

4) **If you need to meet with someone, go to their office (or place).** That frees you from "playing host or hostess" and allows you to leave when the meeting is over.

5) **Write tomorrow's list.** Before you leave the office, write down everything you have to do tomorrow. Don't wait until the next morning. You'll panic. There's a sense of being in control when we know what's happening the next day. Having written it down, we can leave it at work, and not worry about it at home.

These are simple techniques that have been proven quite effective in helping you manage your time. The key, once again, is consistency.

Define other habits in the workplace and at home that you'd like to change. Be creative and adventuresome as you decide how and what needs attention.

ALSO . . .

Learn to delegate. Convince yourself that it's not necessary to do everything yourself.

Several months ago I underwent neck surgery. For weeks I could not bend my neck. My eyes were the only things moving from my neck up. And they moved straight to the floor and saw every crumb, piece of paper, and fuzz ball!

I learned some important lessons during this time of recuperation. One of them concerned the art of delegating. I asked for help doing the things I could not do. I got the help I asked for, but not always in MY time frame and in MY way of doing things.

It was a difficult choice at first, but I DID choose to accept all the help I could get and adjust my thinking about how and when these things should be done.

The point being: Decide which things you are willing to delegate, then decide to be happy with the results. Your way is not the only way.

Don't be afraid to say "no". You can't say "yes" to everything without spreading yourself too thin. Decide what you must do and what you want to do, and say "no" to other requests.

Get unpleasant things done first. If there's an unpleasant chore facing us, we tend to procrastinate ~ even if it's something that needs to be done. Go ahead and tackle these items. If it's too large and overwhelming, divide it into smaller chunks. (For example cleaning out a desk may seem like an unbearable activity. Why not take a drawer a day until the task is complete.)

Set priorities. **Decide what's important and what needs to get done.** Do these things first. This can be accomplished by making a daily list. I like to have a "home list" and an "office list." After seeing on paper what needs to get done, I then prioritize each item. And if I don't get it done today - I move it to tomorrow. (Remember that YOU are the creator of this list. You can change it as needs change. The important thing is to make your list!)

Stay flexible. **When things don't go according to your plans, don't worry about it.** Understand the nature of time and these self-management principles, but stay flexible in your planning.

Avoid regrets. **Instead of worrying about what you did or what you did not do in the past, realize that regrets are just a part of life.** They are not bad unless you allow them to hinder your future. We can't go back, but we CAN look back and learn from the past. And we are always free to change the future.

TIME is a paradox. We never seem to have enough of it, and yet we have all there is.

As you learn to master your time, you'll also be mastering your life. In doing so, you will accomplish more and gain more satisfaction from the things you do.

Your quality of life will increase as you accomplish more and positively impact the world around you.

Take Time To:

Think. This will renew your mind.

Play. You will stay young.

Read. You will learn new things.

Help Others. You will grow.

Laugh. It decreases your stress.

Daydream. New ideas will be yours.

Plan. This helps restore balance.

Worship. It puts all of life in perspective.

Learning

To

Listen

I know you believe

that you understand

what you think I said,

but I'm not sure you realize

that what you heard is

not what I meant!

3

We are judged by the way we listen!

Do you agree with that assessment? It's been said that good listening habits are the basis for all positive human relations.

It is believed that one's self concept is lessened when talking to a poor listener, and improved when talking to a good listener.

How do listening habits affect husband and wife relationships? Child and parent?   Employee and Manager? Friend and friend?

Listening is how we usually take in information. In fact, we use it more than reading and writing combined.

Even so, it is the least understood method of communication. We often confuse "listening" with "hearing".

How many times have you said to your child (or your husband), "Did you hear what I said?"

Actually we mean, "Do you know what I said", "Do you care what I said", "Are you listening?"

Hearing is the physical ability to transmit sound waves from the eardrum to the ear. **Listening** is putting understanding to that transmission.

And by the way, being "hearing impaired" is a legitimate physical condition. Being "listening impaired" is not!

Do you HEAR me?

Having defined "listening" quite adequately, let's explore some reasons why we don't.

Reason 1. <u>We don't want to.</u> That fact is important to acknowledge. Furthermore, by choosing NOT to listen to everything, we are protecting our sanity.

We are being bombarded with thousands of messages per day. We couldn't possibly concentrate our energies into all of them. So we become selective in what we give our attention to.

Reason 2. <u>We simply tune out.</u> According to research the average person speaks at about 150 words per minute. The brain can process about 500 words per minute.

Now if I can process an additional 350 words per minute when you are speaking to me, then that leaves plenty of time for me to "go somewhere in my brain" while you talk - so I'm tuned out before you know it.

Reason 3. <u>We don't understand what's being said.</u> Words can be transferred from one mind to another. Meanings cannot.

In the training sessions I lead on communication skills, I share this astonishing fact based on research: ***Over 70 percent of what we say is misinterpreted by the receiver.***

Can you believe it?

(Well, actually I can when I think of some of the conversations we've had in the Wood House.)

As most of us would agree that our listening skills could and should be improved, we need to also realize that the purpose of listening is to **understand** the communication, not necessarily **agree** with it.

Reaching clarity of understanding in the workplace leads to enhanced communication and supportive cooperation. Morale is improved and job commitment is increased.

But it reaches beyond our working environment. In our hectic daily living, we also need to make clear connections with those we love. Becoming a good listener can greatly impact the quality time we have with family members.

God gave you

two ears

and

one mouth.

Guess He intended

for you to listen

twice as much

as you talk!

When asked the question, "How do you know when he/she is not listening?", these women gave very targeted answers:

"He's reading the newspaper."
"I hear the computer in the background."
"The T.V.'s too loud."
"His eyes were closed."
"She looks like she's somewhere else."
"There was this blank look . . . ."

But you see, listening involves a sender **and** a receiver. If the sender is not satisfied with the manner in which the receiver is receiving, then listening is not at its best. *So tell that to Him!*

How would you rate YOUR listening skills?

Do you:

Keep eye contact? I know you've heard it said, "I don't have to look at you to listen to you." BUT, having good eye contact is critical to good listening!

Give affirmation?   It is important, as well as an effective listening tool, to give affirmation to the speaker to confirm your understanding of content. This can be done verbally by saying "I understand what you are saying" or "Yes, I see", for example. It can also be done by a nod of the head signifying that you are "tuned-in" to the conversation.

Listen with your body? An effective listener looks like a listener. A listening posture is one that is slightly tilted towards the speaker. This gives the appearance of being drawn into what the person is talking about.

Ask questions? By asking questions you show interest and clarify your understanding of what's being said. Asking questions also helps the other person clarify what's being spoken.

It's also very helpful during a conversation, to repeat some of the content. Use phrases such as, "Now let me make sure I understand what you are saying . . ." or "Do I understand you to mean . . ." or "Am I hearing you say . . .". This procedure allows time to verify and clarify what's being said by both speaker and listener. This is particularly helpful during conversations when misunderstanding is evident.

It is also helpful and interesting to realize that people have developed a particular pattern to their listening approach. Some people are naturally more facts oriented. So when they listen they are quick to pick up on facts and concrete information.

Others have more emotional tendencies. When they listen, they tend to listen with "emotional ears."

Improving your listening skills will help you build positive relationships, as you value the spoken word *enough to listen to it!*

The trouble

with people who

don't have much to say

is that you have to listen

to them too long before

you find out!

Exercising Your Body

Age brings

wisdom and character.

<u>I'd rather have</u>

<u>cute buns!</u>

COUNT <u>ALL</u> THE CALORIES!

Many women who sit at their desks throughout the day just don't seem to realize that lots of calories can be burned by many strenuous activities that do not require physical exercise.

Here's a partial listing of the calories burned per hour and the exertion required:

250   Pushing your luck

107   Jumping to conclusions

 75   Bending over backwards

150   Climbing the walls

500   Making mountains out of molehills

350   Running around in circles

175   Throwing your weight around
        (give or take, depending on your weight)

If God meant

for me to eat

celery and carrots,

He wouldn't have

given me tastebuds!

4

One of the best reasons I know (and what keeps me at it) for exercising, is the storehouse of energy it gives.

A key quality in being that dynamite of a 21st Century Woman (almost), is a huge reservoir of energy.

You can greatly increase your energy level through a well-designed (not complicated) exercise program. It takes some organization, some time management, some *movement,* and plenty of self-discipline.

When I say "not complicated", that's exactly what I mean! Exercise can be as simple as walking! Brisk walking for 30 minutes a day *is* exercise.

The benefits to an exercise program are too numerous to list here, but consider these few:

Exercise clears your head. You become more creative and alert in your thinking. Sorting through things and analyzing situations will become easier.

Exercise keeps you healthy. When you follow a consistent exercise program, you are less likely to catch colds, viruses, and experience fatigue.

Exercise increases self-confidence. There are many issues we face over which we have little control. You *are* in control of what you do with your body. As you begin to feel better through consistent exercise, you will also feel better about YOU!

Exercise helps you lose weight. You become overweight when you take in more calories than you burn. Nothing else burns up calories and fat as quickly as exercise. Combine it with a low-fat diet and see quicker results.

Exercise keeps you aerobically fit. In order to be at your best physically, your heart and lungs need to be strong. Consistent exercise helps keep you breathing and pumping in a healthy way.

Exercise is also good for: high blood pressure, good posture, reducing thighs, relieving anxiety, helping you sleep, improving concentration and memory, cellulite loss, pms, cholesterol control, relieving heartburn, and preventing tooth grinding and back aches.

Now tell me. Can you honestly think of ANY good reason why you should not be exercising?!?

As you consider an exercise program, think about this; Do you *wish* to exercise your body or do you *want* to?

There's a difference between WISHING and WANTING. *When a wish becomes a want, you will do what needs to be done to accomplish whatever you were wishing for!*

83

Getting in shape often depends on just how tight your clothes are, how flabby you feel, and how tired you've become.

When you feel lousy enough, you'll usually do something about it. When you acknowledge the fact that you DO want to feel better, look better, have more energy, be in better shape, then you will do the things it takes to get you there.

The desire is as important as the exercise itself!

You want it! You crave it! Let's do it!

Here's the plan:

1) **Start small.** If you haven't done it for a while, exercise can seem overwhelming. Be realistic. Don't try to go from doing nothing to being a gold medal winner. Start small with a goal of gradually increasing your exercise time. You might also try breaking it up. Exercise for 15 minutes at lunch and another 15 minutes when you get home.

2) **Find an exercise buddy**. This support system is what keeps a lot of people going. Many people like company, so they set exercise goals together.

Accountability is a factor here too. If someone else is counting on you, you're likely to show up. There are some women, however, who prefer exercising alone, but set goals with someone on a similar program.

3) **Experiment.** Try different exercises until you discover what works best for you. You should enjoy what you are doing, or you won't stay with it! Also use variety. You can combine activities to keep you interested and motivated. Walking today and bicycling tomorrow gives you a change in your routine.

4) **Be consistent**. Behavioral scientists say that it takes about 21 days to develop a new habit. Consistency is the key to any effective exercise program. On some days you will be tempted not to exercise because of lack of time to complete your entire program. Just do what you have time for. I believe that consistency is more important than the amount of time.

And . . . Remember to be flexible! There are days when you just don't want to do anything. If you've been consistent for a while, take a break. No exercise or diet should be so rigid that there's not room for a diversion every now and then.

Every time I try

to lose weight it keeps

finding me!

Visualize how

good

The New You

will look

and feel!

Do you know what your skinny friends are doing?

They're:

Taking the stairs instead of the elevator and escalator.

Parking farther away from the door.

Walking more and riding less.

Drinking lots of water.

Eating low calorie snacks.

Being more active in general.

Exercising Your Mind

You know you're

losing your mind

when you stop to think

and forget to start again!

5

There have been many studies relating physical illness to psychological roots. Many sicknesses are influenced for better or for worse by the state of our mind.

That's not to say that we can prevent or cure every illness through mind power. However, the latest research makes it clear that the mind is a healing tool like no other!

There's much being promoted today about taking care of the body. Rightly so. Physical fitness is very critical to good health and a positive outlook on life.

But there's more. Could we be missing another important dimension of health by not exploring how to keep our minds in shape?

Furthermore, by exercising your mind, you begin to stretch your thinking skills and come up with creative solutions to complex problems.

Your state of health (mental and physical) is improved because you are focusing on positive and creative challenges by giving yourself a mental workout.

Before exploring a "mind exercising routine", let's take a look at what generally happens when we allow our minds to plant and grow negative thinking.

According to cognitive therapists, many people who think they are dealing in reality are actually wallowing in negative thinking which has become grossly distorted.

Here are some characteristic mind distortions:

Exaggerating: Do you overestimate the size of your problems? "I'll never make it through the day," and "My whole life is falling apart" are examples.

Many people wildly exaggerate the size of the problem and at the same time underestimate their ability to deal with it. These same people are quick to jump to conclusions, believing the worst in the situation.

Ignoring the positive: Some people focus on the bad in the situation, ignoring the good. "Yes I enjoyed the shopping day, but the house was a wreck when I got home."

Personalizing: Some people think everything revolves around them. Now this is a major distortion of the facts. "People kept looking at me because I've gained weight."

Either/Or thinking: I find many women guilty of this one. "If you're not going to clean the kitchen the way I clean it, don't bother."

Overgeneralizing: "I can't do anything right." "Nobody thinks I'm any good".

Jumping to conclusions: "I haven't heard from the test results yet. It must be bad news."

After reading these, you can see that negative thoughts begin to sound alike after a while. They really are alike. One characteristic of negative thinking is that it is generally wrong.

After one develops this pattern of negative thinking it tends to become automatic. These thoughts have a way of just leaping into your mind. They do not show evidence of thought and logic. In fact most of the time, they don't show evidence of thinking at all.

The point is to put your mindset in a realistic perspective. Consider the positive and the negative, then determine what's real.

In order to do this you're going to have to "exercise your mind" out of those negative thought patterns.

Exercise #1: Work on becoming aware of your negative thoughts and feelings. Counting them may help. Try using straws or transferring coins from one pocket to another. This will give you a heightened awareness of your negative thinking tendencies. When you become aware of a problem you can work on it.

Exercise #2: Counteract those negative thoughts. Ask yourself questions such as, "So what's the evidence that I'm no good?" and "Am I forgetting my good points?". Also ask yourself if you are exaggerating or overgeneralizing or perhaps jumping to conclusions.

Exercise #3: Give yourself affirmations. These are personal positive statements that can send you in a new direction. You might begin these affirmations with the words "I am . . .", "I can . . .", or "I will . . ." . Write them. Read them. Repeat them often. Put them on your mirror, in your car, on your refrigerator.

Here are examples:

I will face today with confidence and enthusiasm ready to handle any problem with calmness and assurance.

I enjoy life, people, and myself. I plan to live each moment to the fullest.

I have the power to choose how I will react to each and every situation today.

When my son Lane was just a toddler, I taught him to say " I like myself" all during the day. I still remember our journeys through the grocery store aisles with him squealing to all who passed us, "I like myself. I like myself." We got lots of laughs as he learned the important lesson of being content with his uniqueness.

You too are a wonderfully unique individual with capabilities beyond your wildest dreams. It's important that you like yourself ~ and tell yourself often!

Other Mind Exercises:

1) **Pay attention to new ideas.** Keep track of things you'd like to remember by jotting them down in a small notebook. I carry a composition book with me just about everywhere I go. I like to remember words, phrases, and ideas that make me laugh or give me reason to reflect.

2) **Think about new and different things.** Step out of your comfort zone of thinking by reading about or acting upon an idea that is not typically "you". You develop mind power as you expand your thinking horizons.

3) **Be receptive to the ideas of other people.** New ideas are fragile. Listen positively to them. Be willing to try out something new and different.

4) **Observe everything.** Study things around you   Pay attention to distinguishing features. Notice beauty.

5) **See the humor.** Life has lots of humorous moments. Practice looking for them. This helps you relax and is stress-relieving.

6) **Know yourself.** Be aware of your strengths and weaknesses. Set self improvement goals and monitor your progress.

You know you're losing

your mind when you

finally get it all together ,

but can't remember

where you put it!

And remember:

Your body and mind work together! In one study researchers found that people who got an hour of aerobic exercise three times a week, performed better on memory tests than those who didn't work out.

Exercise increases oxygen flow to the brain. With this supply of oxygen your memory skills are improved. Exercise also reduces stress, which can inferfere with memory and the ability to think rationally.

More Mind Shapers!

To think straight, sit straight.

A hunched over posture can interfere with the thinking process. The brain needs more blood than other organs in the body. When the upper body sags, the spine is curved and the arteries passing through the spinal column to the brain can not do their work effectively. Holding yourself straight, with your head back and your chin tucked in, helps you think better.

Remember to remember this when trying to remember.

If you are trying to remember where you placed your keys, a letter, hairbrush, etc., try associating the lost item with pictures, gestures, or a physical experience. Recreate the experience in your mind. For example: I had it in my hands when I walked inside, then answered the phone . . . . . .and put it on the counter.

Presenting A Positive Image

You never

get a second chance

to make a positive

first impression!

6

You only have one shot at making a first impression, so make it count. Your voice and your ability to communicate are certainly essential, but the **visual image** seems to be what counts most when someone first meets you.

The image you present, is not only the clothes you wear. It's the way you come across to the other person. What do people "sense" when they see you? What signals to you send to others communicating with you? Do they perceive a person with much self-confidence or one who is nervous and insecure?

The way you are groomed and the clothing you wear are big contributors to this powerful and positive image.

According to an article in *The New York Times,* "The impression people make on one another is based 60 percent on their appearance, 33 percent on the way in which they speak and 7 percent on what they say." If your clothing is sloppy and your appearance disheveled, your professional image is certainly at risk.

Now this doesn't mean you have to be a raving beauty or invest in designer clothing to succeed in life. It does mean that you should dress neatly and appropriately. For business; skin-tight and low-cut is out, along with too much dangling jewelry, dirty blue jeans, torn stockings, and unkempt hair.

Keep your appearance low-keyed and dignified. When others look at you, you want the image they see to instill confidence. Knowing you are well groomed, boosts your self confidence as well, whether you are delivering a sales pitch or trying to get your staff motivated. How you feel about yourself always shows through!

Along with your personal appearance, your work environment is also a contributing factor to the image you present. If co-workers see piles of paper spilling onto the floor or a stack of used coffee cups on the edge of your desk, they make judgements about YOU.

This visual image suggests disorganization and lack of confidence. Why should people trust you with "their business" if it looks like you would lose their paperwork under a stack of unopened mail?

Realizing the importance of a positive image will help you be proactive, as well as give you an inner sense of security, in the way you "come across". Keeping the importance of your image clearly in focus will aid you in sparking others into action too!

Successful women stand out and fit in at the same time. Although not always striving to be liked, they do want to be remembered favorably. Often, especially during a first encounter, people don't have the time to actually figure out your motives and intentions. They form their impressions of you by looking at the outside and making assumptions about what's on the inside. They take you at face value. It's your privilege (and responsibility) to establish that value ~ and do it quickly.

People base their perceptions on what they see. Although you can't actually control other people's feelings and perceptions about you, you can control *what you show them.*

Successful women stand out and fit in at the same time!

Enter a room with purpose
and confidence.

As you interact with others,
remain interested, involved
and caring.

Let the image you project
be the Real You!

There are no hard and fast rules on the specific behaviors needed to make a favorable impression. Just remember to "design the impression" that fits your immediate circumstance and best suits your purpose. An initial impact that might fit one circumstance may be all wrong for another.

Some tips to ponder:

1) *Determine the impression you would like to make in a certain situation.*

2) *Figure out what you need to do or avoid doing in order to make that positive impression.*

3) *Then follow through.*

By controlling all your actions, even seemingly small and insignificant ones, you can positively influence other people's perceptions about you and greatly influence your chances for success.

It's been said, "The best place to find a helping hand is at the end of your arm." You possess all the tools you need to create a dynamic and positive image!

How you feel about yourself always shows through!

Steps to creating a powerful image:

Smile: This is the single best thing you can do to help others feel comfortable in "approaching" you.

Look people in the eye: Relaxing your facial muscles will help you communicate sensitivity and interest.

Shake hands: Clasp palm to palm establishing a firm grip. This demonstrates authority and interest in building rapport.

Stand tall, slightly tilting your chin upward: This gives power to your physical presence.

Pause and pay attention: Using pauses throughout an encounter helps you think and maintain a strong presence.

Wear clothing to fit the occasion: Think quality, not quantity. Darker colors present a more authoritative image. Dress to look current rather than trendy.

Groom yourself well: Pay attention to details such as your fingernails, jewelry, and shoes.

Breathe deeply and slowly. This will help you project your voice. Breathing deeply and slowly also helps you project an image of calmness and confidence.

Listen effectively: Show interest by your facial expressions. When appropriate, refer to something said during the course of the conversation.

Show your sense of humor: Don't be afraid to laugh and enjoy the situation. Displaying a sense of humor often helps others feel relaxed and comfortable. Don't overdo it, but have a good time. Also, stay away from ethnic jokes.

Stand when others enter a room: Maintain a relaxed posture and keep your arms loose at your side.

Ask questions: This lets others feel involved in the conversation and gets you the information you need.

Make an entrance: Pause and relax as you enter a room. This allows time for you to size-up the situation, also giving you a "power look".

Be positive: Successful people think well of themselves and others. As corny as it may sound, optimism prevails at the top!

Winning People To Your Way Of Thinking

7

We all have encountered people who are difficult to get along with. For whatever reason, they argue; they complain; they make impossible demands.

Some time ago during a training session dealing with how to handle difficult people, I was explaining the negative characteristics of a particular style of behavior. As the participants and I were discussing these traits, one such "difficult person" erupted with the words, "I am tired of hearing this. I am not power hungry and hard to get along with!" With that she stormed out of the room leaving a group of bewildered co-workers, conceding that was *exactly* who she was!

It takes real patience and empathy to respond to difficult people. There are some strategies you can use to win people over and to help them see your point of view.

In order to get along with these difficult people, first be aware of yourself and your feelings in the situation. That can be a tough order, especially if you are upset. But if you can give up *your need* to control or to be right, the other person will begin to relax and start listening to you.

A lot of determination and a spirit of respect for yourself and the other person is needed in order to do this. It also takes practice. *The more often you step out of your point of view into the viewing point of the other person,* the easier it will become. You will begin to notice some real benefits to this approach, as you are actually putting yourself in control of the situation.

If you are in a managerial role (at work or home), and need to deal with a difficult person, try these methods to help you avoid or lessen confrontation:

1) **Give praise and honest appreciation where it is deserved.** Acknowledging the positive helps work with the negative. Notice when improvement happens. Your encouragement can go a long way in correcting negative behavior.

2) **Help the other person save face.** Embarrassing or belittling another person never helps them improve.

3) **Criticize gently.** Make the fault seem easy to correct. Help the other person come up with ideas to improve the negative behavior.

4) **Avoid an argument.** The only way to win is to NOT argue. That's getting the best of it!

5) **Try honestly to see things from the other person's point of view.** When others realize you are doing this, they feel that their ideas are important too. They will then be less likely to argue.

6) **Be empathetic with the other person's ideas and desires.** Discuss their feelings about the issue in question. Appeal to their nobler motives.

7) **If you are wrong, admit it quickly and emphatically.** This helps the other person realize that you are also vulnerable to making mistakes.

8) **Show respect for the other person's opinions.** Don't tell another person that he/she is wrong. Respecting someone doesn't mean you necessarily agree with what they are saying.

Try first

to understand,

then it's more likely

you'll be

understood!

In order to gain an understanding of what's expected from those with whom we work, I posed two questions. Here are some of the replies I received. Use them as insights to what may be expected of you in the workplace.

To the "Boss"

What do you like in a secretary?

Quick thinking

Able to locate needed information

Good public relations skills

Punctuality

Pleasant and optimistic

Confidentiality

Trustworthiness

Someone who plans ahead

Professionalism

To the Secretary:

What do you like in a "Boss"?

Someone who: Explains exactly what he/she wants

Keeps me informed

Plans ahead

Considers the feelings of others

Provides needed details for the job assignment

Returns calls

Exhibits fairness

Is consistent, kind, considerate, and proactive rather
than reactive

It's important also to remember that regardless of job title, description, and position in the company . . . each individual person wants the opportunity to:

- *have and express an opinion*

- *be treated with respect*

- *ask "why"*

- *say "no" and not feel guilty*

- *make mistakes*

- *change his/her mind*

- *ask for assistance*

- *have his/her needs be as important as the needs of other people*

- *be treated as a capable human being and not be patronized*

Proactive ways to deal with difficult types:

The Aggressor:

This person enjoys intimidating and threatening others. Avoid arguing. Listen to everything they say without responding in an emotional way.

The Underminer:

Don't overreact to their sarcastic and devious ways. Focus on the issues, disregarding the sarcasm.

The Unresponsive:

Ask open-ended questions to the type who finds it difficult to express his/her ideas. Learn to be silent and give this person plenty of time to say something. Be patient and friendly.

The Egotist:

Make sure you know the facts since this person tends to "know it all" and feels superior. Agree when possible. Disagree only when you know you're right.

Remember these very important words:

- 6 important words: **I ADMIT I MADE A MISTAKE.**

- 5 important words: **YOU DID A GREAT JOB.**

- 4 important words: **WHAT DO YOU THINK?**

- 3 important words: **IF YOU PLEASE.**

- 2 important words: **THANK YOU.**

- Least important word: **I**

People Winning Tips:

Be patient and tolerant of others.

Do not expect people to be perfect.

Accept the differences in others.

Be sure you want to understand others.

Look for the good in all people.

Learn to love the unlovable.

De~
Frazzling
Your Life

Don't sweat the

small stuff . . .

and most of

it is!

8

I've discovered something about stress. It doesn't stay at home when I go to the office, nor does it stay at the office when I leave to go back home. It follows me wherever I go! Call me brilliant, but I DID notice this.

Many of us store up stress like air in a balloon, accumulating it until we just can't handle anything else. These negative stressors build up day after day after day until . . .BANG! Your balloon pops over some seemingly insignificant event. Don't you just hate it when that happens?

Imagine this scenario:

You get a last minute "assignment" on Friday. Since you have to finish this report by Monday morning, it is necessary to cancel the family outing planned for the weekend. You just don't have time . . .

You know they'll be disappointed and it's an unreasonable demand you've been given, but what choice do you really have?

The rumor going around the office is that they're going to promote someone in your department to a higher paying position.

You really need that raise if you and your spouse are going to be able to qualify for the new mortgage you want.

You'd love to tell your supervisor what you really think, but . . .your thirteen year old needs braces . . .and you still haven't started that college fund.

Get the picture? Here's where you notice the first

Stress Puff!

So, you cancel the weekend plans and try to explain it to the kids. All they know is that, once again, you've let them down. (Of course they don't realize it's for them)!

Your spouse is understanding, in a sad sort of way. Wasn't there a time when you promised each other that your careers would never get in the way of your family life? Well, that was a long time ago. You know all of this will blow over eventually.

Stress Puff.

You work through the weekend.

You live on coffee and quick snacks for two days. You ignore that burning sensation in your stomach.

Stress Puff.

When you present the report to your supervisor on Monday morning, instead of a smile and a thank you, the only response you get is a memo to fix two typos in the report before noon that day.

OK, it's no big deal. Yes, it's a bit inconsiderate, but what can you do about it?

Stress Puff.

You go to lunch early. A fried chicken sandwich and chips rush to your stomach, while complaints about your autocratic supervisor rush to your mind.

Stress Puff.

After you get home, you decide to go for a walk just to regain some composure. A half mile from the house, you twist your ankle and have to limp back home.

Stress Puff.

Your children don't seem very interested in your swollen ankle. After all, you're the "promise breaker."

Stress Puff.

Your spouse helps, but then points out that maybe the problem is that your ankles aren't used to supporting the extra weight you've gained over the last while.

Stress Puff.

The next morning on the way to work you stop for a cinnamon danish and coffee . . .

Stress Puff.

. . . and lock your keys in the car . . .

Stress Puff.

. . . so you pay fifty-five dollars to a locksmith . . .

Stress Puff.

. . . and get to work late . . .

Stress Puff.

. . . and you hear that your supervisor has been looking for you . . .

Stress Puff.

. . . to tell you that they won't be needing that report after all . . .

Stress Puff.

. . . and oh, by the way, someone in another department was given the promotion.

Major Stress Puff.

The stressors continue to build.

Late one evening, after a long and tiring day at work, your child asks for help on a math problem. You agree to help, even though you're so tired you can't even think. (You still feel guilty about not spending time with your family.) You get stuck – on the problem and . . .

POP !

You just explode. You say things and do things you shouldn't. You completely lose it!

Now your family doesn't understand how this happens over a silly ol' math problem. But you see, it wasn't just the homework. It was the accumulation of small stressful events that had been building for quite some time. Then – then – then – you just couldn't take any more, so you explode.

If you and I don't deal with stress – as it occurs – on a daily basis, then we will experience this scenario happening over and over in our lives.

I can only please

one person today.

TODAY

isn't your day!

Stressful Truisms:

~ Cashiers may not count your items in the express line, but other customers will.

~ The fancier the restaurant, the smaller the piece of pie.

~ The bar code in the checkout line won't work on items you're embarrassed to be buying.

~ In word processing, the worst typos remain invisible until the printout.

We will explore, in these final pages, some effective ways to deal with the stress in your life. Be reminded they won't work if you don't put some action to your reading. To manage YOUR stress by DE—FRAZZLING your life is the single most important thing you can do for yourself and those you love.

Understand the nature of the stress in your life. When you feel that you are headed for burn-out because of all the demands at work, home, church, etc., remember that all stress is not avoidable.

And yes, SOME of it is actually good for us because it sets us to action! It can heighten our awareness and push us to resolve a problem.

So—trace your stress roots. Be conscious of what is causing the "unusual" stress in your life. Then deal with it. If this stress is something you have control over, decide on steps to overcoming it. Then do them.

If the stress is out of your control and absolutely unavoidable, accept that fact. By this acceptance you are choosing to deal with it.

There is a difference in acceptance and resigning to the fact, which suggests "I have no choice in the matter." Choosing to accept, is recognizing that the choice is in your power.

And . . . if things get really difficult ask for help. It's no shame, and in fact it's commendable to realize you need help. By asking assistance, you'll more than likely find that others have experienced a similar stressful problem.

Before looking at some STRESS BUSTERS let's take a look at what may come your way if you don't handle the stress within you.

Now I could fill pages and pages with negative stress symptoms, but that would be terribly depressing. We'll just let it go with these "few":

upset stomach, racing heart, excessive sweating, dizziness, hot flashes, cold chills, stuttering and stammering, stiff neck, stiff back, stiff everything, headaches, twitches, forgetfulness, ringing in the ears, high blood pressure, shallow breathing, cramps, clenched teeth, joint problems, hives and warts, heart problems, and yes—even dandruff!

Oh yes, and then there's anger, anxiety. and depression!

Now tell me. Don't you want to do something to avoid this pain and misery?!?

This is as bad

as it gets,

but don't

bet on it!

De-Frazzlers:

- **Slow down and relax some during the day.** Take a little time to get comfortable and feel peaceful. These occasional breaks will clear your mind and help you think about pleasant things. You'll also find that this calming exercise is well worth whatever it takes, to do it. Taking this break will empower you with fuel and freshness to deal with turmoil.

- **Choose to deal with negative attitudes.** These disruptive thoughts cause "brain drain" and siphon your energy. Besides that, worry and frustration take up so much of your precious time. You could better use this time on problem solving or positive interaction with others. Practice replacing these negative intruders with positive and pleasant thoughts.

- **Find something to anticipate.** This may be an outing with family or friends. It could be a needed get-away for you to have some private time. Whatever it may be, the practice of anticipation stimulates zest and the zestful person has more energy to deal with the unexpected – which of course, IS expected.

161

- **Take slow deep breaths**. Slowly breathe in as deeply as you can through your nose. Then quietly and peacefully let the air all the way out. Do this at least three times a day. Getting the stale air out of your lungs helps you feel more energetic.

- **Exercise.** Now this has been mentioned in every other chapter. Must be pretty important, huh! A fast-paced workout for 25 minutes a day can do wonders for your physical condition AND decrease negative stress levels. The payback from this investment is well worth the time and energy involved doing it.

- **Close your eyes and think Happy.** As corny as it sounds, this practice will help calm you and help you relax. Remind yourself of your priorities in life. Think about what really matters to you. Maintain a proper perspective.

- **Give yourself 10 minutes. . .** after entering your home in the evening – to change clothes and "regroup". Don't talk to anyone before you've had this time.

- **When things get really tough, confide in a friend.** It's healing, talking with someone who understands.

He/She Stress

Towels: One of you leaves them crumpled, the other doesn't even want the tags showing.

Air: One of you is a fresh-air nut. The other is a cold bundle of shivers.

Soap: It's all one of you needs. The other drags in a stockpile of accessories.

Toothpaste: One of you squeezes it in the middle, the other thinks that's sadistic.

Pancakes: One likes them extra thin. The other likes them semi-fat – and at MY house, the third likes them thick and silver dollar sized!

Morning: One is an early riser. The other thinks that if God intended for "man" to enjoy a sunrise, He would have scheduled it at 9 AM.

I've used all my

sick days, now

I'll have to

call in dead for

the SECOND time!

Research From:

Emrika Padus, Ex. Editor. The Complete
Guide To Your Emotions And Your Health. Rodale
Press. Emmaus, Pennsylvania: 1992

Derric Johnson. Lists. The Book. Vol. I and II.
Y.E.S.S. Press. Orlando, Florida: 1993 and1995

Pete Fagan and Mark Schaffer. The Office Humor
Book. Harmony Books. New York, New York:
1985

Cindi Wood, through her company CREATIVE DIMENSIONS, offers seminars to help people grow through creativity and change.

With a variety of programs ranging from team building to stress management, her audiences include those in businesses, government agencies, schools, and churches.

For information about the following seminars, you may call (704) 739-8950 or Email cawood@shelby.net.

Building Your Team
It Must Be Stress
Learn How To Listen
I Love The Kids, But Hate The Stress
Teaching With Style
The Frazzled Female
*Page Me If You Need Me – I'll Be In
  Cyberspace*